MW00630220

Heidi Rose Robbins

WILD COMPASSION

Also by Heidi Rose Robbins:

This Beckoning Ceaseless Beauty
Sanctuary

Wild Compassion

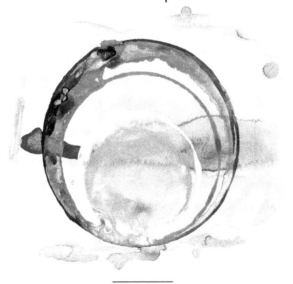

Heidi Rose Robbins

© 2018 Heidi Rose Robbins

Heidi Rose Robbins

Wild Compassion

All rights reserved. No part of this publication may be reproduced, stored in a retrieval system or transmited in any form or by any means, electronic, mechanical, photocopying, recording or otherwise without the prior permision of the publisher or in accordance with the provisions of the Copyright, Designs and Patents Act 1988 or under the terms of any licence permitting limited copying issued by the Copyright Licensing Angency.

Published by: IngramSpark

Design by: Wyoh Lee

A CIP record for this book is acailable from the Library of Congress Cataloging-in-Publication Data

ISBN-10: 0 99107 893 6

ISBN-13: 978 0 99107 893 6

Los Angeles, CA

For
all
who
gather
in the name of
LIGHT.

Wild Compassion

Heidi Rose Robbins

A Letter to My Readers

Dear Friends,

Welcome. I am so glad you are holding this book and spending this moment with me. I am grateful for you.

Poetry, at its best and most potent, is a doorway into love and presence. It pierces us and lands us in the now. It opens the closed heart and reminds us of the beauty of our ordinary lives. One well chosen word evokes laughter or tears and releases us from old pain, fear or sorrow. Poetry allows us to see ourselves anew with more hope, compassion and purpose.

Poetry has, in fact, always set me right. It points to the tiniest beautiful thing and says, "Look here. Breathe here. Spend some time here and you will emerge refreshed." It stirs the soul and beckons us to give the best of ourselves. It shines light on obstruction as says, "Love this. Lift this into the light and you will see you life anew."

Always, poetry at its best is an invitation to live a richer, more deeply felt, engaged life.

I read a poem out loud every morning. I let it wash over me. I feel how the words transform despair to possibility, fatigue to whole-heartedness, and lethargy to hope. I invite you to do the same. I invite you to memorize a line of poetry and let it infuse your day.

I hope these poems and prose touch you in unexpected ways, open doors within you and remind you of your inherent light and goodness. Let the words soften your heart so that you may live with an ever increasing tenderness towards yourself and all you meet.

Big love,

Heidi Rose

Promise me
you'll read one or two
of these poems
aloud.

Contents

FOUR: SILENCE

FIVE: WOMEN WHO GATHER

SIX: BECOMING THE SONG

ONE

The Burning Ground

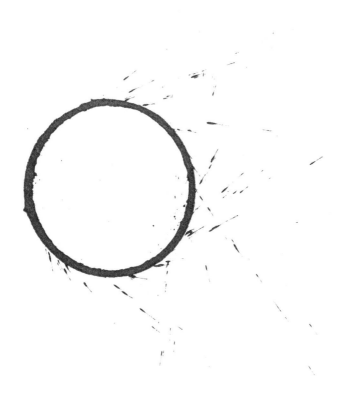

Burn

"Love is the funeral pyre where the heart must lay its body."
-Hafiz

The contour of doubt,
The shape of not enough,
The crumple of imperfection,
This ungainly, awkward body of fear,
I lay now on the funeral pyre.

Burn away the weight of perceived lack.
Burn away the sadness of never enough.
Burn away the need to be the first, the only, the brightest star.
Burn away the critical eye.
Burn to ash the one that withholds love for fear there is a
diminishing supply.

Set me ablaze with the resplendent beauty of the world.
Fire me with the wonder of the gifts others give to light my way.
Ignite in me the fierce lover of all,
the one who stops at nothing to see another thrive.

Burn this body of doubt and fear
and leave me the smallest ember of blazing truth.
I will tend that flame,
the flame of the purest, most radical love,
the eternal flame,
my human heart.

Freedom Carver

Heart, heavy.
Cloak of futility, mine.

I curl up,
give up,
offer up
an endless sigh.

Brimming tears,
no where to go,
driving anyway,
a glimpse in the rear view mirror.
All I see is lost time.

Today foolish
for having a dream,
done, wrung out,
full up to my eyes
in the repetition
of a responsible life.

Carrying some
old pain
yet to put down,
the ancient familiar
whispers in my ear.
"This is who you are,
serious girl.
This is who you are
refusing light's kiss.
This is who you are,
costumed, festooned,
wanting to be something you're not."

Ah yes.
This place.
Its intractable grip.

And still.
I know this.

I'm a freedom carver.
Words are my sharpened edge.

This far from grace,
reaching for my pen
is like reaching for the moon,
but I will summon
every last shred of hope
to fly in the face of this sorrow.

Michelangelo set loose
the soul in stone,
cutting away what imprisoned life.

I will write
again and again,
carving through
the hardened crust
to the molten lava core,
with a head lamp and an inky pick axe,

and
the certainty
(yes, tasted)
that everything
that isn't love is just waiting
to become it,

melting into the center
of itself.

I will carve out what isn't mine,
filling pages with black ink
mouthing the words
that require the breath
that move the body
somewhere new,

and burn away the dross
as I stand as
love,
at the center of the page,
watching
well worn sorrow
eaten
by this fiery dance.

Scratchy, Itchy and Out of Sorts

I am scratchy, itchy and out of sorts. My skin doesn't fit. I am wrangling a 3-year-old tantrum that keeps slipping out of my grasp and laughing at me. I am too young to be old and too old to be young. I am tired of everyone and craving even deeper intimacy. I love what I do and resist it every day. I am grumpy and broke.

Everything feels slightly off. Emotions are running high. There are whispers in every corner.

I have three dear friends who have just fallen deeply in love with new beautiful men. Thank God for that. It's a kiss of springtime. I'm breathing them in.

How can one go from leading such a composed and orderly life to feeling slightly crazed and raw? Why doesn't my glorious healing survival kit work? I have a kick-ass skill set of ways to bring peace. Even if I could open it—the lock is sticky—everything in it feels inadequate.

I've never had a migraine but my emotional body feels like one.

Even as I write this, I'm laughing. And I'm crying. I always laugh and cry at the same time.

I'm wise but I don't have all the answers. I can help you, but often I can't help myself. I can love you truly, madly and deeply, solely because we're alive together at this moment and it's the only thing that will save us—but I often can't truly, madly, deeply find that love for my own crinkly self.

I'm a teacher, an astrologer and an artist. It's the artist part that's the most self-confrontational and probably the scariest. But I think I'd rather be writing that in my occupation line right now—the kind of artist that disappears in her studio for days, eats ritz crackers and emerges only when the work is complete.

We emptied out our studio and I love it. I can see the sunlight on the floor. I stole my husband's desk. He was nice about it. I like it better. Mine was an old school teacher's desk and I no longer love the vibe. I'm selling it at an impromptu garage sale next week if you want it.

Pleasant will no longer do. Nor will polite. I think the stakes are too high.

I am still ferocious about not splattering my mess on others. I just want to tell you about it, to see if it rings any bells. I'm all about taking responsibility for the burning ground within. No one is to blame.

I'm growing up. I'm growing stronger. I'm growing more clear. I'm asking more of myself and others. It just looks messy right now. And as awkward as it feels, I'm going to let it be messy as long as it needs to be.

This morning, I wandered around the kitchen in my ratty sweater getting lunches ready for the kids muttering lyrics from Beyonce's Lemonade. "Cause I slay. I slay…" Yes, stop a moment and picture that. Not sure why I'm telling you. But perhaps to give you a glimpse of the glorious awkwardness of growth.

Let be.

Hungry

I order a glass of wine.
Red.
No white.
No,
Red.
Pinot Noir.
It's on special he says.
And then a salad.
Caesar.
I'm sitting at the bar,
writing.
It's dark, romantic even.
Everyone is talking with
someone.
I'm talking with the page.

A salad.
Yes.
That's enough.
Don't order more.
You're a woman.
It's not okay to be hungry.

Oh but I'm hungry.
I'm hungrier than I've ever been.

How about that curried Cauliflower?
The women two stools down ordered
and split it.
They pick at it,
leave half.
I want it all.
The waiter is curious

about my hunger.
I can tell.
What are you writing?
A poem,
I say.
I watch the word land.
It's unexpected.
"Wow."
Then silence.

Fuck it.
Another glass of wine.
I don't mind sitting here by myself.
I love it.
I feel good.
I worked hard today.
I'm tired
and I'm hungry.

Yes.
Still I am hungry.
What's that plate
with the slab of meat?
It looks good.
I need protein.
I've been drained for years.
I'll have that.
I feel better even before I
take a bite.

I am scrawling words across the page.
They are not neat.
They are edgy and wild.
Dessert menu please.
"Of course," he says.

Now he is full of wonder.
What woman eats and eats
satiating every desire,
alone?
Me now.
I do.

Two slabs of chocolate torte,
caramel,
walnuts.
Wine still to drink.

Yes.
Yes.
Chocolate.
Poetry.
Wine.
I am unapologetic.
I am round bellied ecstatic.

I may never
go hungry
again.

The In-Between

Extremes have always been comforting to me for their clarity and stark contrast. The all or nothing approach has made sense and doesn't leave time to ask questions. The caffeinated, driven, scramble up the mountain-side way of life has been my way.

Funny then that I now find myself in a world of soft edges and blurry next steps—a world of increasing stillness and humbling uncertainty. I am living in the in-between, the middle, the soft center. I am firmly lodged in the realm of the unknown.

At first as this blur begins, I think I'm just terribly depressed. I'm uncomfortable with the pace of my life, the lethargy and lack of direction. In moments, it feels terrifying. I lie in bed at night and think 'Will I always feel this way? Am I just getting old? When will I know what's next?"

Though I have been uncertain in my life before, I have never been here.

But I write these words now because I begin to sense a glimmer in the darkness. I sense a new and tender trust with this unknown territory. In moments, I feel spacious. I can only do what I can do and I can't do a lot right now. Shall we call it surrender?

To-do lists aren't making sense. The day begins to unfold in a more organic way. I find myself sitting at the kitchen table and loving my little blonde boy's vivacity and wanting to steep in it. I look at my daughter and drink in her laughter. There is time for this. Imagine that.

I could never imagine that. There is time for a life to unfold in an organic way. There is no rush. This is the realm of quality, the realm of the soul. Quantity cries out at every turn. We do not always have to answer.

I am deepening. I am like a field, now fallow, but being nourished and prepared for a new planting. It takes time. My fallow field must sit in the sun for days. It must soak up nutrients for weeks. It must be whole unto itself no matter its state of fecundity. It must realize its beauty even in its emptiness.

This is the necessary in-between, the quivering at a threshold, the vast quiet without end. This is a time of true perspective. This is living into what matters, what is material, what has substance.

The space in-between matters. The space in-between you and me, the gaze that we exchange, the words that reach out and touch us or pierce us or soften us. The search matters—the search for meaning, for unraveling the mystery, for the heart of things. What is felt matters. And it's okay to feel it all, allowing it to move through, allowing it to change us. The unknown matters. It is not yet defined. There is magic in that. Anything can emerge.

It comes down to this. I'm discovering that this in-between place allows me to be more deeply with myself and with you. It allows me to feel you. Before I can move into my next work, I want and need to feel you—to feel us—to feel our heartache and our yearning to live more fully expressed.

Close your eyes and meet me here. It's time out of time. You can arrive in a single breath. There is nowhere to be but here, with one another, in the thick of the in-between, in wonder, in awe.

13

A Gentler Way

It is raining. Los Angeles always needs a good rain. It needs the reminder that the sun is not always out and sometimes you have to wear a raincoat. It needs an outward dance of the blues so that everyone living here has some relief from the constant dance of inner fret and outer blaze.

I have been wrestling for the last 24 hours. It's one of those inner dances where one wants to throw in every towel owned and move somewhere remote. It's a momentary "what's it all about anyway?" It's a quiet voice whispering for comfort and a louder voice bashing the need.

Sometimes I feel very courageous but mostly I feel like huge parts of me are still hiding. Sometimes I feel like blazing the trail and pulling out all the stops and other times like I'm quite happy to trod the marked path. I wish I were the kind of person that got a little giddy by getting lost and losing sight of the trail and trusting I'd find my way back. But mostly I am afraid.

I think I'm afraid of major thresholds but I walk others through them all the time. I know I'm terrified of loss. And I'm still way too formal and would like to keep loosening up.

Also on a more concrete note, I'm living a little like this:

Tiny pieces of my right front tooth keep flaking off because I grind my teeth at night like a grizzly bear. I won't wear my mouth guard because I hate it. My dentist will fix my tooth but not without silent reprimand and absolutely no guarantee it will last more than an hour.

When I type, I attack the keyboard. I would bet it wears out in record time. I would bet if I were a key on my keyboard I would be begging for mercy. I would wish I were a Q.

My morning alarm sounds like a trumpet fanfare mixed with heavy metal. I lurch out of bed sure that something has gone terribly wrong. I have to sit still for a minute just to reduce my heart rate.

I have been late 10 times in my life. Okay, I'm making up that number but it's something like that. I am never late. I am sweating in the car, biting my nails, cursing at stoplights but I am rarely, rarely late. I arrive 10 minutes early and sit in the car. I arrive half an hour early and walk around the block. I have sadly passed this on to my daughter who now starts to crack every knuckle in her hand if it looks like we might be late for school.

I wake up in the middle of the night and remember 3 people I was supposed to call the day before. I begin to silently punish myself for not doing so. I open the notes section on my phone and add to the on-going list. It brings me great joy to delete notes. It rarely happens.

I am the parent chair of a big fundraiser at my kids' school but every-day I think "I should be doing more. I'm not doing enough. Everyone must think I'm a slacker."

My husband loves to quote the movie Spinal Tap where Nigel Tufnel, the guitarist, proudly points to the volume knob on his amplifier and says, *these go to 11*.

Get the picture? I live life at 11.

Anyone else? Can I get a hallelujah? I know this "living at 11" isn't everyone's particular flavor. But perhaps most of us can relate to a sense of how life doesn't stop these days and how it takes a tremendous amount of will and discipline just to take care of ourselves.

Most of this noise and fury isn't even self generated. The volume of the election is beyond 11. The stories of how we are treating one another throughout the world feel like a daily Tsunami. We live in crisis. We're absorbing it all and think there must be something terribly wrong in our own small lives. We're all steeping in this intensity together.

So today you find me ready to do something about it. I'll put it this way: I'm quietly registering for the school of gentler living. I wish to be a student of living well. I am curious how it would feel to consistently turn the volume down, take a step back or say no more often. Most days, I feel I am a failing and flailing and am doomed to repeat freshman year again and again. Some days I feel I know a thing or two.

I notice more these days when I am spinning out. I notice how I clench my jaw. I notice when I'm saying yes and inwardly shouting no. I notice how happy I am when I have a day with absolutely nothing on the calendar. I notice what it feels like to breathe deeply and quietly and fully.

I'm finally even making some doctor's appointments and listening to my body. That feels good. That feels like I am stopping to mother myself instead of fathering my way through.

I'm wondering what the holidays would feel like if I entered them softly and with curiosity instead of swinging a shopping bat with a 10 foot check list in my hand. I am 100% certain that if I typed more lightly, changed my alarm to a lovely quiet piano, walked around the block once a day and maybe stopped to admire something beautiful, my life would begin to change. Yes. I want to live more gently, to receive the grace that is everywhere, but only if I pay attention. I want to sit with myself without agenda. I want time to slip through my fingers like water and trust nothing has been lost.

Oh, and I'd like it to rain a little more often.

Wild Compassion

You know the days
when you're better left alone
and if you happen to be in
a dark corner
in a dark room
all the better for you
and everyone else,

the days when
not even sugar or
a stiff drink
or your drug of choice
makes a shred of difference
in the landscape of sorrow?

Or is it rage?
Or fear?

Whatever your flavor of closing down
curling up
slamming shut
however you
refuse to shift,
deny the light
that just wants to
cast a splash
of hope across your cheek.

You know the days
when all you do
is sit
and stare,

can't move
your face
to anything
but slack?

Lack everywhere.
Lack of hope
money
motivation
mojo.

Doesn't matter
how far I've traveled
down any spiritual path.
Equanimity
poise
objectivity
flung out the
window at dawn.

This life is a ride, people.
Anyone who preaches
from a pulpit
and refuses to
acknowledge the unstoppable
raging current
is not to be trusted.

The ones to listen to
have a wild compassion
in their eyes
that comes
from riding that current
on a makeshift raft

crafted from
loss and resurrection.
Best thing to do
with a day like this
as far as I can tell
is muster up a nod to it,
a generous nod
to the stranger walking through
from parts unknown.

If you can find the words
or even just lift your head,
invite him in for
coffee black.

Ask him why he's come,
what he hopes to find here
in this
wild, wild
wilderness.

Listen up.
He'll mumble,
shed a tear.
He won't make sense.
Listen closely.

Say your farewells and
watch him walk into a fiery sunset.
Watch him burn at the center
swallowed by the flames.

Lay your head on your pillow,
and exhale.

Give it away,
the stranger,

your day,
all of it.

Die into the darkness
that will swallow your pain
with its fierce love.

Set down your honorable load.

Then trust
this:
Morning light
will touch your cheek.

You need only turn
ever so slightly toward it.

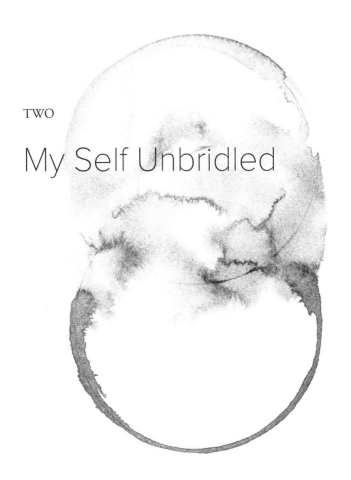

TWO

My Self Unbridled

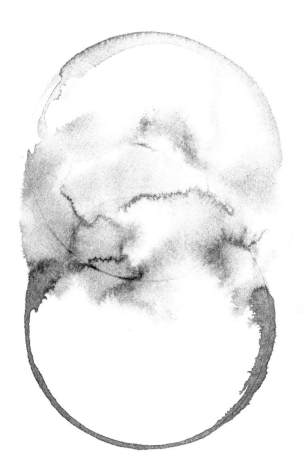

Grace

An unexpected peace
in the middle of the day.
Nothing that needs doing.
No one to knock
for at least an hour.

Ever so carefully,
her hand finds a pen,
first time in a year and a day,
and sudden tears for the relief of pen to paper.

Her head buzzing.
Her heart beating as for a lover.
Her skin on fire.

The page yearns to know her.
Its blankness invites her truth.

Here, it says,
Be only as you are.

Here, it says,
Lay your cares.
Unfurl your yearning.
Tell the not so beautiful
truth.
Here
be only the you
that is
naked
revealed
hungry.

She scrawls quickly,
covers the page and refuses order.
She gulps the air like water,
shudders and shivers
and even laughs.

She calls out to the white landscape,
"I am not yet done.
I am alive and yearning.
I am beginning again in so many ways."

She insists on circles and cycles
and timelessness,
refuses upstoppable linearity.

She says,
"I feel like springtime though I walk
disguised as winter.
Don't let me fool you.
I have wise words but I feel so young.
I need to be held firmly.
I do not want to walk alone
though I may behave otherwise."

Now,
her breathing begins to steady.
She finds herself hovering
outside the door to her very self.
She sees and feels the windows
flung wide and the
great door opening.
She finds herself
returning to the center of
her home.

She sits on the throne
at the hearth of herself,
and remembers whom and what she loves.
She, the fire, at the center of her life.

It is quiet,
ever so silent
for a time.

Then, she lays the pen
on the page
and blesses them both
grateful for the
unexpected
peace that
carried her
home.

I Can No Longer Be Contained

(to be read aloud)

I can no longer be contained.
I'm busting out like a storm.
I'm the weather baby
and it's okay
to rearrange,
shake it up,
rain it down
like a torrent,
like a lightning strike,
sweet spring rain.

I can no longer be contained,
because I am breathing now
all the way down to the belly
of who I am,
and I am tired of constraint
of holding myself back,
tied up,
tied down,
wrapped in doubt,

Retraction,
Contraction,
Subtraction.

I am pacing like a pregnant rhino
and I've been pregnant for a long time.

It's birth time baby.
It's the season of birth.

I am a woman in my prime,
like a number that cannot be divided.

It's time to own it,
Full out time to

unfurl,
uncurl,
dance it out,
dance it in,
love.

I can't stand still.
Don't want to.
It's not about composure.
It's about composing.

I am breathing now
and speaking now
and my throat has become a
tunnel of love.

Can't stop the truth,
it's pouring out,
and the truth is beauty
but sometimes hard to hear,
because we are used to our complaint.
We are married to our fear.
We are enmeshed in our anger.

And that's life, right?
It's all good until we are tired of
what defines us,
what confines us.

It's all good until we want something more
that doesn't contain us,
that doesn't constrain us.

I am pacing like a wild thing
who is hungry for her natural habitat.
It's calling me now,
lush and green
and howling and free.

Free to be.
You got it.
Free to be me.

My Self Unbridled

You call me
on my birthday
at midnight.

You've been calling
all night,
you tell me.
Where have I been?
You were worried.

I just 18,
giddily drunk
with friends,
pour myself
into the room
reaching for the
ringing phone.

Just before
my best friend says
"Don't,"
I grab for the receiver
and laugh a
buoyant hello
to discover
you
at the end of the line.

I begin to choke
back tears the moment
I hear your voice.

I know now
something will
forever change.

Your love requires
my perfection.
I am to be the child
you never had
forever.
I am to walk a narrow
path of precision
and goodness for you.

But your love has teeth.

I want to be what you want me to be.
I want to,
never,
not ever,
for a moment,
Let you down.

I make up a story.
We went out.
My friends and I.
We ate burgers.
No, everything is okay.
Do I sound funny?
Just tired.
Just tired.
Try not to blur the words.
Try not to cry.
Try not to feel 10 years old
when I am a college girl now.

Something crumbles
when I say goodnight.
My friends
puzzled by the gravity of my reaction
comfort me.

But I am caught in a life and death
struggle to hold
myself as whatever you need
to love me.

"You just had a drink
on your birthday,"
they say.
"This is what you are supposed
to do in college,"
they say.

And maybe the love in their voices
And maybe a breath in and a breath out.
But suddenly a crack,
splintering my past self,
revealing the first
taste of a life I want to live
uncircumscribed,
flying in the face of another's
disappointment
to risk my
Self
unbridled
in the world.

Breaking Up With Myself

I'm breaking up with myself today. I'm letting myself know that though I can see that I'm trying, that I'm giving it my best effort, that I'm earnest and all that—hells bells, trying is not enough. This is what I'll say to myself: "You're just too, well, serious, dower, glum. You're too single-minded, formal, somber." I'll probably be firm but with a slightly apologetic tone. "So maybe I'll see you around," I'll say as I exit. Perhaps I'll cry a bit from the intensity of the moment but then, well, I'll skip away, free.

I know I'm worth the effort but sometimes it's just time for a chapter to end. I'm always telling everyone to move on, clear space in their life for something juicy, yummy, potent, sexy, free and delicious to enter. I say, "You can't keep allowing the same bad behavior. Clear the decks!" I say, "End it now. Be bold. Believe in a fresh chapter."

So if I'm going to be doling out such snappy advice, I have to follow through, yes? I have to draw a line in the sand. I have to break up with my rule-follower, time-constrained, people pleaser, ears around my shoulders, crinkled brow self. I have to tell her to skidaddle. I might walk her over to a mirror and tell her to have a look. "Do you see what's going on, oh furrowed one? Where is your 10 year old laughing self in there? She has high-tailed it up and vanished." I know the mirror business is somewhat drastic, but sometimes you just have to tell it like it is.

I know the broken-up-with *me* might feel sad for a time, might eat too much sugar or drink too much wine but I suspect she will eventually chill out and explore some new ways to live. She might go from 'this sucks' to 'I don't want to stay in this pit' to 'maybe some things have to change' to 'wow, this feels good" to "Um, actually change is freedom, baby." Who knows? Maybe our paths will cross again down the line and it could all be very, very good.

Meanwhile, it just has to happen. I'm saying good-bye to my sour-puss self. I'm making room for something else. I'll listen to new music and let my body move like water. I'll take a few long, directionless walks. My backyard hammock has been gone too long. Mostly when I wake up, I want to feel like my whole body is as free as my daughter's giddy laugh that cascades out of her on a daily basis. Maybe I won't get out of bed in the morning until my whole body feels like a wash of light.

The Inspired Life

I will admit that my first thoughts, post morning alarm, are not inspiring. My first thoughts have something to do with calculating how many more minutes I can stay in bed and still manage to make the kids' lunches, wake them up, get them breakfast, take a shower and get us all out the door in time for school. I usually can swing another 12 minutes under the blankets. But even buying myself those 12 minutes doesn't do a great deal to increase my morning joy factor. Those 12 minutes include trying to find a position that alleviates the pain in my shoulder, then unclenching my jaw which has been clenched, much to my dentist's dismay, all night (and no I won't wear that god awful plastic mold to save my teeth from shattering like an Ancient Greek Monument).

Next, I begin THE LIST. I list errands for the day, yes. But I also list books I haven't written yet, things I should feel guilty about and character flaws that may never be resolved. I list friends who are probably mad at me because I haven't been in touch or haven't been in touch enough. I enumerate all the ways the house is falling apart and how I don't know where to begin and even if I did, how we don't have the money to put towards that right now. Then I make a note to myself to check my bank account balance.

So. We're really just about 4 minutes after the alarm sounds and it's already decidedly not inspiring. It's bleak. Eventually I execute the inner order and hoist myself out of bed. For awhile, in my life, I would sit up, put both feet on the floor, take a deep breath and remember the things for which I am grateful. Note to self: try that again sometime. It might help.

Once out of bed, I make the bed. I didn't used to do that. However, I've become convinced that to live an inspired life, it's better to turn the chaos factor down to a dull roar and create a little breathing room through beauty and order. So by way of folksy encouragement, I would suggest making your bed when you get up in the morning. You'll feel better and you'll breathe a little easier.

Breathe easier. It really is all about breathing. I'm pretty convinced. This inspiration thing is about choosing what we are *inspiring* throughout our day. Are we breathing bleak or breathing beauty? I know it isn't easy to breathe confidence and joy every moment. That's why you've just heard how my day often begins. But it's only when I admit to the bleak, self-critical, lethargic, caffeine addicted wretch I often feel I am that I can begin to whisper to myself about beauty and possibility. Otherwise I know I'm a fraud and no matter how much I'm breathing, when I talk I sound like a Charlie Brown adult with an incoherent trombone voice.

The truth is once we admit our heaviness, once we admit feeling old or tired or washed up or ugly or not enough, then something else begins to flicker. We've let our darkness out into the light of day and it begins to transform. Then we can remember who we truly are.

Once I do this, I remember—I am a hopeful person. I am a soul who loves to grow. I recently said to myself when I was in a relatively good space—"well, let's have a look at next year. It's about that time. And I actually LOVE having that conversation. What is possible? How do I want to feel? What could the year hold?" And without too much angst, I said, "I want to feel whole-hearted. I want to live in a whole-hearted way." Then I asked myself, "well, Heidi Rose, what does that mean?"

What that means is when I say YES, it must be a whole YES. It must come from fullness. It must come because I have inspired. I have taken a deep breath and I have seen my life, situations and yearnings clearly and I have determined that at this moment in my life, yes, I do want to step forward, have coffee with a friend, chair that event. And I want to do it with every part of me.

Otherwise, no. No. Otherwise, I experiment with what the word no creates. For sure it can create closure, immobility and isolation but it can also create an unknown, magical, sparkling space.

What if this year were the year that everything was put on the table, "Do I feel whole-hearted about this? Does it bring me joy?" What if the answer was no and that was ok? What if I just headed down to Goodwill with all that half-heartedness? Then, what if I followed a beautiful, organic whisper? What if I could begin to hear a whisper that is a true voice of self love? What if I listened? What if I deeply listened? What if I *inspired* that?

Then, my loves, I might find my stride, living a life that makes me feel alive, that is true to my bones, that awakens my very whole heart.

This Magnificent Body

My body says
hold up there
and pulses a pain
in my abdomen
where something has grown hard,
closed in on itself,
not wanting to budge.

I won't listen
to the rhythmic pain
until she puts on the emergency brake,
stops the train,
says put me in bed now and rest.

You have no choice,
no voice
in this my friend.
We've traveled too far without fuel
and we're stopping on these tracks
in the middle of nowhere
so don't try to run.

Only then in that quiet
do I feel something silenced long ago, wanting to be heard.
And first the fear,
the floods and fathoms
of fear that this pain
has too long been neglected,
and just like my grandmother, I,
dead,
too young.

But then the listening
and orange flowers that kept blooming
from my belly as a breathe,
my body in my bed,
giving it all away
to the turquoise of the earth
while I rest in awe
studying renewal.

When did I stop listening?
"This magnificent body," my friend says.
"But I'm sick," I say.
And he says,
"This magnificent body, when did you leave it behind?"

When did I?
When did I run away
to climb the mountain alone,
with effort, strain,
a full brain as my only companions.

But now,
communion,
reunion
with
this magnificent body,
stunning transportation,
vehicle to deliver and receive
every moment's bliss,
all mine.

For a precious time.

I-You

My father
thinks
mostly
of infinity.

He uses an
infinity symbol
as a capital "I"
to remind us
we are more
than we think we are.

If a waitress asks him
what he wants for lunch,
"Wisdom"
is his response.

In Fargo, North Dakota
in the 70's
he had a radio program
which always ended
with the same farewell:

"If you know who you are,
you'll know what to do."

And dad says
who we are
is infinite.

And I,
well,
I am my father's daughter.

I say
Who we are is
Radiant,

Who we are is
Luminous,
Shimmering,
Blinding light.

My father asks for Wisdom.
And I ask
how I might
be more fully
what I know I am,

How I might be
that radiance
in this finite world
in the density
of this body.

Then I breathe
and remember
this
body.

This vessel that holds the light.
This kind form housing my heart.
This hearth for the inner fire.

This is the body
where I
love myself into the light I am.

This is the body
in which I love you
into the light you are.

My father
thinks
mostly
of infinity.

I think
mostly of
how to be love
in this body
more often,

How to love
the mess of
myself
more completely,

How to love
all I have
been given to love
without hesitation
or complexity.

My daughter
got it right when
she learned to say
I love you.

She forgot the word love
and just said

I-You.
I-You.
I-You.

Well,
Can it be that simple?
Can this moment
in this body
be the practice?

I-You.
I-Me.
Here.
Now.
Infinitely
Radiantly
Completely.

The Quivering

If we but make friends
with the quivering,
the subtle and not so subtle
shaking of the body
and all its parts,
letting go
of what we've held onto
long enough,

If we but soften our grasp
on who we have always been,
to make room for
what can be
knowing not
what may appear,
knowing only
the quivering,

And I ask,
Is not some part of us
always dying?
And I ask,
Are we not everyday
in some small way
reborn?

Then, just as the
wild animal shakes
off the fear of attack,
we too can shake
off the fears that
want to eat us whole.

We can walk
barefoot in the woods
with a quiver of arrows,
cautious of what
still wants to ensnare us,
but alive with the
light emanating
from our newly
trodden path.

Are we not path makers?
So we are.
Are we not path finders?
So we are.
Do arrows not quiver
before they are loosed into the world?
Then so must we.

Finally,
we are archer and arrow
at once
sprung into the wind
carried swiftly,
silently,
precisely,
to our
very
heart,
pierced and present.

THREE

The Wilderness

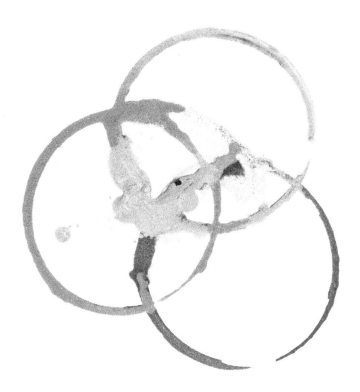

Kali on Hold

It is buried
some where at the back of my throat,
and under my left breast,
and in the deepest pit
of an invisible second stomach.

It is metallic
and cuts at everything
I half do,
disgusted with wilting
normalcy.

I am a vagabond yogini
trapped in a suburban smile.

I am a tattooed
20 something hipster
tiptoeing through life
at twice that age.

I press the mute button
just before it gets juicy.

My mother fucker
is lodged behind a tonsil.

I am furiously holding myself
back,
talk a good game
and live bound and gagged.

I am Kali on hold,
terrified, restless,
imploding.
What's a girl to do
who is here to be fierce
but finds herself setting the table?

Do not ask me for the story.
This is how it feels.

Even the word
rage
is unacceptable,
too hot, unpredictable, dangerous.

The Tasmanian Devil?
My favorite as a child
but a wild, flailing tantrum,
never in my life.

Time to break plates.
Jackhammer.
Spew.
Discover no.
Howl.

Let this page
teach my body
the YES
of opening to the mess
of everything,

no longer tentative
but fiercely devouring,
fiercely demanding,

what is beautiful,
what is alive,
what is true.

Thinking About Writing

It's now been 2 hours and 52 minutes since I first started to think about writing. I start at 5 am lying in bed. Dylan calls out for me which is rare these days. I plod down the hall. He wants me to curl up. I know his bed isn't as comfortable as ours and I know Andrew is getting up for an early morning interview. Dylan comes back with me and falls asleep again immediately. Now I'm probably up for good but refuse with all my might to really be up. The inside of my right hip hurts, something in the muscle. I've been grinding my teeth again. I can feel it. I'm parched from 2 glasses of wine last night and I'm too hot in these pajamas. All that and I haven't written anything decent in weeks. I plump my pillow and dive back in. I refuse to wake up. It's summer.

But if I'd only get up, I could write in the romantic early hours when everyone who has written anything seems to write because the house is quiet and the thoughts are fresh. I could make a cup of tea and sit in our big comfy brown chair and begin. But, hell, the house is full of guests. Kate had Zoe spend the night. My niece Aja is sleeping in the studio for the summer and Andrew is doing his early morning interview in the kitchen. Why bother? Two minutes pass. If I were to get up and write, what would I even write about?

Now Dylan kicks me and I curl up into my favorite sleep position. I look like a chimpmunk praying in a fetal position. Enough said. I don't need to get up. I don't have any appointments for 4 1/2 hours.

Shit. I should just get up and write. But what will I write about?

I'm a fraud. I keep talking about writing a book and I keep not writing it. I know I shouldn't wait for inspiration. I'm unhinged and pacing through my days. Some might call that relaxing. But for me, it's unhinged and pacing. Let's add 40 visits to the refrigerator every hour and then we have a more complete picture. Yesterday in one hour, I ate hummus and carrots, skittles, guacamole and chips, a dried pineapple chunk, a bite of an old potato latke and a Trader Joe's vanilla creme cookie.

I wish I had a generally stronger constitution so I could kick my ass out of bed and start writing. Maybe I should start kick boxing every day and then write afterwards. I'd get in amazing shape and then would have the momentum to fall into the page.

I flop onto my back and kick my leg out of the covers. I can never fall asleep on my back. This signals defeat. Now I'm in worry position. I like our gold ceiling. At least I worry and look at a gold ceiling. I can't get out of bed to write this morning because I have to review what isn't working in my life first.

What's wrong is I'm too self-involved. The world needs my attention. If I put my attention and love and goodwill out towards others, everything will fall into place. Time spent sending love to those who need it most is time well spent. Maybe writing books is a thing of the past. Maybe it's all about action and putting my money or lack of it where my mouth is. Maybe I should try to do good in the world and stop trying to make a name for myself. What's that all about anyway?

Lately I don't love my Leo rising. It's too egocentric. Too prideful. It needs too much attention. Screw that. Why am I writing anyway? What do I hope to accomplish? Who needs another book about the Heart?

I sit up a little from my strictly prone position. Well, it wouldn't just be any book about the Heart. It's not going to be a self help book. It's going to be Hope on the page and an investigation of a mystery and a reminder that we are all spinning the same old carcasses of questions in our head without invoking a deeper answer. It would be worth writing about. Even if no one read it. Maybe it's a book I just need to write for myself. Hilma af Klint, a Swedish painter born in the late 1800's, worked on about 150 paintings for 20 years of her life that she only showed to 5 women during that entire time. She was painting them for a new temple. That's all she knew. And she knew she didn't want them shown until at least 20 years after her death. So, she worked on these paintings in secret and filled pages and pages of notebooks about her process. Today it's all on display at the Serpentine Gallery in London.

She inspires me. Reading about the lives of artists inspires me. Living the life of an artist is something else. It's lying in bed at 5 in the morning and trying to get out of bed to write.

Okay it's now after 7. Dylan is even getting out of bed before I am. There's nothing to do but heave myself out of bed into the great unknown. I'll make a cup of tea. I'll eat something. I'm hungry. The house is still relatively quiet. Dylan will build legos for awhile. Where's my computer? Here it is. On empty. The girls watched *Hunger Games* last night. I hope Kate was okay watching that. Not sure that was the best decision. I plug the computer in and sit down. Dylan calls out. He needs some toast. Done. The gardening guys have just arrived. There goes the mower. Not so quiet. But dammit, I'm going to write. How do I feel? Delete. Delete. Delete. Why does anybody ever do this?

There. Maybe I'll begin here. That feels okay for now. Yes, that's worth exploring. I'm feeling a bit better. Oh I like that. That's exactly how it feels. Maybe I can do this. It's 8:30. Isn't writing the best?

I Want to Feel Everything

That's saying something
from the girl
who bites her nails,
holds her shoulders around
her ears
too many years,
refusing to risk exposure.

That's saying something
from the woman
still too intimate
with unceasing apology.

I want to feel everything,
stay with the feeling
until its spent,
I'm spent,
until its had its way with me and I'm grateful it has.

No matter how raw, angry, sexy, sad,
elated, craving, petty, crazy, mad,
I want to feel it.

Because I've been so careful,
so very, very careful.
If you ask me what I feel,
I may not even know.

No wonder my best girls are lightning rods
for bolts of feeling.
They cry pools of tears
until I'm standing in a lake of their allowing.
I thank them.

They dance like a wildfire,
burn and rage.
I watch in wonder
and feel the heat,
yearn to burn.

They carve clarity
and opinion and want
with precision,
perfect and strong,

because they are fighting
for the richness of their life and mine.

But, I can no longer buy a ticket to the show,
recount the day's events after the fact.
Can't tell a story instead of living it,
making up what
I might have felt
if I were truly there to feel it.

It's time to feel everything.

I am irritated, exonerated, exhilarated.
I am shy, sad, fly, bad.

I am sexy, sultry, sensual, soft.
I am raging, parading, cascading.

If you're talking to me,
you're talking to the weather.

And if you don't like what you see,
just wait a minute.

It's all passing through
in full splendor.

I'm a
full force of nature baby,
and that's just how it is
now.

Flying in the Face of Fear

I am traveling to Denver, Colorado,
tucked into seat 28E,
the middle seat,
ignoring the inevitable take-off.

These moments pre-flight are always the same.
My breath quickens.
I try not to cry
as I bid good-bye
to all I hold dear.

Struggling to appear calm,
I wildly summon faith.

Oh, this complete surrender,
when a body must sigh away
imagined horror to make room
for something larger,
when all is risked to welcome the
nascent, tender, yet to be.

Only moments to flight and the pilot says
there are storms ahead.

I give myself a little pep talk.
I'm insisting on trust
but my body wants no part of this uncertainty.

Then, quite suddenly,
something snaps,
some inner tension
long held
breaks and from some hidden reserve of courage,

59

in the thick
of my body,
sick of fear,
I hear myself
start to sing like Aretha or Adele
in a riveting, time-stopping voice
that there are always storms ahead, my love,
so walk on.

We're speeding down the runway
and I'm belting it out.
Now aloft, I'm singing
to every traveler on the plane,
to my daughter,
my little boy blue son,
my husband lover.
I'm singing large and loud,
setting myself free.
I'm a god-damned R&B singer
flying in the face of fear
and you better believe I'm
Walking on.

Six Crows and A Butterfly

I am 5. I am Trouble. That is, I am playing the role of Trouble in Madame Butterfly. Trouble is a boy but my father is the director of the Fargo-Moorhead opera company and it's easier to just cast his kid. He is the Stage Director. David Martin conducts the orchestra. I spend many early years counting the seats in the theatre, playing hide and seek with my brothers, getting yelled at for being too loud. I've followed my father around through the dressing rooms, listened to him give copious notes to actors, watched him sing the entire operas along with the singers from the lighting booth. I've watched him excited, passionate, furious. I've watched him inspire a stage of 50 in the opera chorus to give everything they have.

Now I am Trouble. Trouble doesn't really appear until the very end. The story goes something like this: An American Naval officer, Pinkerton, falls in love and marries a Japanese woman during World War II. He leaves Japan when his war duties are over and marries an American woman. Meanwhile, the Japanese woman Cho-cho has his child and has never fallen out of love with him. Pinkerton returns with his American wife a few years later and discovers he has a child and wishes to bring him home. He doesn't realize that Cho-cho is still deeply in love with him. Just before he comes to get the child, Cho-cho sings a heart wrenching aria to Trouble, commits suicide behind a screen and leaves Trouble for Pinkerton.

So I stand playing Trouble and Cho-cho holds me and sings of her grief. She then leaves me blindfolded, hands me an American flag and goes to end her life. My father actually plays the role of Pinkerton in this production as well. He's dressed in white when he returns to take me home. He embraces me.

Pictures of the production are taken at some point and many decades later, I will look at one in which my father reaches out to me. He is arriving too late. He is just beginning to register the devastation. He reaches out to try to stop something that cannot now be stopped.

My own father's mother died when he was 10. He was never told she was dying only that she was sick. When they told her she was dead, he ran across the room trying to barrel through the door of her bedroom. They would not let him in to say good-bye. They thought it was better that way. I cannot even begin to understand the loss. How has it lived in him? How will it live in Trouble? What does my dad—what does Pinkerton—think about as he holds me? His motherless self?

*****

I wake early worrying about money. I'm doing no good tossing and turning and not breathing in bed. I get up and decide to clean my office. I step out onto our paint chipped back landing and 6 crows fly overheard. I can hear their wings flap. It's that quiet. Something in my heart lets go and for a moment, vastness eradicates doubt. The natural world always has something to say. I just don't listen or look often enough.

My parents have been calling me to talk about their deaths. My father says some final thing to everyone at Thanksgiving this year just in case. He tells me that he's been blessed to have me as a daughter. He tells Andrew that he has many talents and that they are all synthesizing and that he believes in him. My father tells me, too, that he got a chance to tell Mathew, my baby brother, that he loved him. I guess fathers don't tell sons that enough. I'm so glad he did.

This sounds like my father knows he's going to die. He is an astrologer and without giving astrology a crazy name as a predictive, scary, doom-saying, you're going to die, fortune telling mess, I will say it's looking like a very rough year ahead for the whole family. So, I understand his impulse.

I personally don't think he will die. And strangely, I don't think he thinks he's going to die either. But he's always one to take precautions. And so he has.

And my mother too calls to tell me that everything will be jointly in my name to make any transfers easier when she dies. And I sit in the Von's parking lot eating fried rice with extra soy sauce and I talk to her about all these important details.

I've spent most of my life trying to shoo away loss. I imagine the worst and then quickly try to shake it out of my mind. These days I've been trying to sit next to it on a park bench. I imagine the worst and then I try to co-exist with it. There are a multitude of stories of what I would consider unimaginable loss. The kind of loss we would say, "How does she live now?" But everyone could tell you 10 such stories.

How do we survive even natural change, even the very natural loss of parents?

A dear teacher of mine tells me the story of being in Portugal in farming country. She is staying with a family. She's taking a walk. She hears wailing. A farmer sits collapsed in a field holding his son, just killed in a farming accident. He wails. He cries. He moans. She says the sounds are not of this world. And then he quietly carries him back to the house.

He let something go fully, bodily, entirely in the very moments of his son's death. He empties himself. I don't know the rest of his story. But though he may have been quiet in the rest of his days, I don't imagine he was frozen in grief. His sound moved something through. He made room for the river of life to keep flowing.

Why am I telling you this?

Six crows fly across my silent backyard this morning. Each time their wings stroke the air, I feel what it is to let something go. Gracefully. And I feel the vastness that holds it all. And I feel all the ripples of loss and how we continue.

*****

I am Trouble. My mother is saying good-bye. I am looking out to an audience—some of whom are asleep, some of whom are crying. My little body does not know loss. Her song sung, her face pressed to my cheek, whispers that some day I will. Some day I will understand the song that can only come from a breaking heart. My father, my actual father, gathers me to his chest. His own loss is alive within him. Pinkerton will take Trouble home. My father will take me home. He will hold me close.

The audience applauds. We go home. We all go home after heart-break. Our lives continue. We wake up—as I wake up this morning. We walk out of doors. And today is the morning of the crows. I hear their wings. I see them disappear and I hear her sing—each note of loss dissolving into light.

Revolutionary in Disguise

(to be read aloud)

I'm a revolutionary in disguise.
What you see with your eyes
is always only half the prize.

Don't write me off quite yet.
I've never worn a sweater set.
But even if I did,
just because I have two kids
and drive a sensible car
doesn't mean
I'm not on fire
with desire
to change the world.

My wild child
who lives just beneath my skin,
well she's something.
She's got a nose ring
and a tattoo on her back.
Her hair is a mane
and a mess.

And beyond all that,
all that what we all look like
chat,
She loves away
all the spaces in between where we feel
our separation
our indignation.
She is keen on eyes,
and stays there

locked in
while everything that isn't love
grows thin.

Her revolution
is the evolution
of the heart.

It's a start
Just to say
Hello Love,

To take
what has fallen apart
and weave
it back to connection,
shedding protection,
creating a collection
of moments
of resurrection.

Breathing life back in.
Reminding ourselves
we are not the walking dead.

We are waking love.
We are waking up.
And we are all
Revolutionaries in disguise.

What goes on behind those eyes?
We're just a lot of love
wanting to give it all,
waiting for some kind of permission
to be that raw.

Well, here it is.
Here it is.
Here
it
is.

Be the first to claim the prize for loving the most
from behind those eyes.

Read my Lips

Bloody Mary.
Sheer Madness.
Rosey Nude.
Pink Crush.

My lips are hungry for color.
Beyonce is in my blood.
I want more than you know.

My lips are full
And mostly naked.
But today I want everything.

I want Beauty,
Courage,
Sexy swagger,
Power and invitation,
Mask and celebration.

Allure and armor.
Sex and commerce.
Back the fuck off
every shade of red.
Come a little closer
every glossy whisper.

I want my body to pulse
with the color of my lips
without hesitation
all of me wanting all of you,
Or not.

No time for any shade
without a statement.
I have something to say.

Yesterday I bit my lip
and it bled for an hour.
How could anything be so full of
blood
passion
pain.

My lips don't hide.
They don't curl in,
retreat.
They ask for communion.
Contact.

Read my lips
and you'll read my mind.

Brave Red.
Ethereal Orchard.
All Fired up.

How do you see me?
How do I feel me?

I've been living
Chapstick
but that chapter
is over.

What are you waiting for?
What am I waiting for?

Light up my
ethereal orchard.
My Pink Crush is making
me Brave Red.
And it's time for a full out
Cherry Symphony.

FOUR

Silence

Silence

Bereft of silence for many months,
I curl in
like a cat on a lap
and purr.

She holds me,
caresses my soft body
loving what is,
kisses my brow,
relieves it of strain.

Now whispers,
quieting chaos,
"Rest in this, love.
Let go.
Sleep in my arms."

The Rain Room

I take two months and quiet down. I take two months and stop, breath, wander, wonder. I take two months and sit with my life without all the busyness and hullaballoo. It changes me. The subtle world is interwoven, in-between and invisible, unless we stop to notice it. But the Subtle World is where all the beauty lies, where peace is a pattern that makes its way into the soil of the earth and grows carefully into all the danger and noise. The subtle world is everything I can almost taste, touch, or smell—but not quite—and still find its current like a warm embrace, something I can depend on. I take two months to make friends with the invisible.

My friend tells me about the rain room at Los Angeles Contemporary Museum of Art. It's raining everywhere at the center of the room but the moment you step into the rain, it stops. The moment you dare to get wet, tangibly soaked on purpose, you step in and you are protected. You are held by light and emptiness and you know there is magic at work. It takes awhile to get used to as we are all so ready to brace ourselves for the downpour, but the moment we walk into the downpour with a full breath of surrender, we walk into a kind of grace. We are not met with what we expect. We are curious again. We think 'How is this possible?' 'How can this be?'

After two months of quiet, I walk out into the world certain of downpour. I empty my life as much as I can and feel certain that when I cross the finish line I will re-enter chaos. And I do. And I don't. The world certainly continues. The pace doesn't lessen. But like a snake, who shed skin and scales even from her eyes, I am seeing something new— A world to be present in.

Observer and participant at once. Wise woman and little girl. Joy looks on. Happiness transpires. The rain room of the world offers us the invitation to walk in wonder, to step forward unhindered and play with what we think is inevitable.

I take two months and quiet down. Now I carry it with me like a secret treasure. I am a new bride marrying her full life with an innocence and curiosity. Everything belongs. There is no reason to hurry. Each moment is mine for its dawning and imminent discovery.

Kin, Skin, Kind

Sometimes when the world erupts and blood is on the windshield or the cafe table or the sidewalk and we can't breathe with the news and we can't see for a minute because all we can see no matter where our eyes land is the fragility of those we love most—the immediate devastation possible in every second. We can't hear because all we hear is our own wail of grief, with the grief of the world so real and so present. And we know it could be even more personal in a flash, and that is terrifying.

Sometimes what happens when the chaos outside matches the chaos inside—sometimes we soften. What has been hidden creeps out into the light of day, unashamed and says, "Yes, sadness. Yes, hopelessness. Yes, fatigue." And it says, "I can be what I am here in the light of this brutal day."

Faces are finally faces and not masks and we see our skin as it is—a delicate, raw layer between the world and the blood and guts of who we are. And if we touch, we touch something that is alive but is dying and we feel its death and must begin in some tiny way to accept it.

When towers fall, when bombs explode, something shatters in each of us, something that hardened over time, became immoveable, became rigid. And something tender blinks and moves towards the light of day. Suddenly isolation cannot win. We have to touch something. We have to touch someone. We have to tell the truth. We have to remember that space is irrelevant and across the globe is also in our veins.

We are blasted apart so we can recognize we are inseparable. There is no hierarchy of pain. Sadness is sadness. Grief is grief. And Kindness is a kinship that reminds us, in every gesture, that we are just that: Kin, Skin, Kind.

In the face of the unfathomable we do our best to melt, expose and recognize that the pain is all of ours to hold. And goodness, kindness, kinship—let us make it all of ours as well. It is ours to breathe, transform and release in each new day.

Invitation

Let's meet by the water where the ocean licks our toes. Let's meet there when the fiery ball of sun reaches as far as it can before its disappearance.

Let's meet without watches, in no hurry, taking time to cross the sand barefoot, the long stretch of sand still warm from a day of absorbing light. Let's meet because we yearn to, because there is no place to be but at this vast ocean's edge.

I'll be there when you arrive. There is nothing to say. Come and stand with me. I want to breathe here with you. The water is a little rough. It shows its colors as an offering. I want to breathe here and feel backwards and forwards over time and rough waters and still be right here with my toes curling in the sand next to your toes curling in the sand.

Hold my hand. I'd like that. But let's not talk yet. Let me feel the hugeness of your hand wrapped over mine, steady and strong. You are stillness and depth. I invite you here because there is little difference in the way I feel about you and the waters. You feel the same.

I never want to know you completely. How can I? We breathe and I wonder what is underneath the water and underneath your skin. The only way I want to be touched is with a touch so full, I cannot resist. The only way I want to be touched is with the sure press of your hand, knowing that you are touching so much more than skin.

Touch me like the ocean would if I walked in and never turned back. Lap against every part of me. Wake me with your chill, the shock of you. Crash into me without apology. I want nothing tentative.

If you meet me by the waters, if you choose to hold my hand, if you only speak if there is something better than silence, if you touch me—-then let it be wholly. I will unfold like the beach we stand on, warm and particulate, endless and surrendered.

That's what I want. To taste surrender and heat. To feel eternity lapping at my feet. To be without time but with you. But to be with the you that is indivisible from the water, indivisible from the depths, indivisible from yourself.

I'm already at the water's edge. I am breathing. I am waiting.

Softer Than I Have Ever Dared To Be

My friend and teacher said: 'Write about Your Genius"

My genius always begins with a breath in and a breath out. It begins with turning inward. It begins when I remember there is a river, a waterfall, a stream of tears that need to be cried and that my job is to keep trying to tell the truth, because every truth peels away an unnecessary layer from my hard working heart. It's something like how gorgeous and bright the sun feels after a downpour. Everything shimmers. I can see a new way.

Look, what I suck at is that I show up all brave and responsible and like I can take anything (and I can take a lot) but then do a desperate dance to avoid the landslide of tears that wants to pour over my body, which will soften it and make it more available to be touched, to meld with those I want to love.

My genius is that I keep trying to be true to the softness. My beloved friend and teacher said, "Think of yourself as a grotto - dark, moist, receiving, quiet, feminine. Let yourself be that tender, that simple. Show up in your yearning. Show up in your sacredness."

Sometimes I am all boundary. I am efficiency in action. I lead the way.

But my whole being yearns to surrender to the waterfall inside and let go, to be sloppy and wet and curious, about you, about me. To not have a single answer. To find the answer with everyone I love.

Sometimes I am hard inside—so rigid, so righteous. No one would know. I want the boundary of the flesh to be no boundary at all. I want you to know me inside out. Where I am hidden there I am a lie. So says Rilke. And I don't want to lie for another moment.

There's a hurricane in my heart that is gaining power and my love is huge. But it will be messy. I want to love in a messy way. I want to breathe in and out and I want you to see my stomach, my beating heart. Any words that hide tears need to be spoken so the tears wash away all the barriers between the simplicity of you and me.

I want to be softer than I have ever dared to be. I want to be so soft I may never find the words to finish this because the waterfall in me is singing.

This Fragile Tower

My father sleeps
curled on his side,
his breathing labored.

It is day three
in this sterile room
of fitful sleep and watchful
waiting.

We will not lose him this time,
but our hearts
sustain an unalterable
crack,
One that lets the light in,
so says Leonard Cohen.

What is precious will fall away
too soon.
All we hold beloved is ours
now
to love.

My towering brothers
suddenly tender,
stay close.
A hand on my father's forehead,
my older brother says,
"This is the hand that healed a hummingbird."

My younger brother,
deep in thought, searching,
impossible to give words to the sea inside.

Divorced 15 years shy of their 50th anniversary,
my mother tells him a story.
"Remember that fall in Ann Arbor?
You left me a note at the apartment.
'Meet me in the Arb.'
I found you in a tree.
You said you were talking to God.
I should have known better then."

We all laugh.
Today this sterile room in this fragile tower
hosts a homecoming,
an unexpected reunion,
filled with hope
and secret promises
given the chance,
to love better,
to love more.

FIVE

Women Who Gather

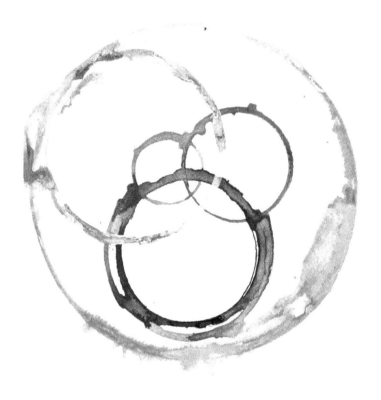

She Skirts the Rules

She will never walk the straight and narrow.
Her hips are wide with care
and her stride leans into
New
Electric
Undiscovered.

She won't stop for
fear or ignorance
barring her path.
She is water flowing around every river rock.
She is fire burning what outlives its time.

She knows what is under her skirt
but never flaunts her power,
just moves with grace that doesn't need words.
The wake she leaves behind says all she needs to say.

She loves what is hers to love with ferocity and tenderness.
Her touch soothes and ignites.
Her love demands that you stay awake.

She celebrates silence,
Works from a still point.
Wholeness pours forth
from quiet eyes.

She skirts every rule,
milks every no into not so absolute,
welcomes rough seas
and finds her song in the darkest hour.

She is resolute and reaching,
Sports a crown or an apron,
Wears whatever disguise she must
to offer
Her Soul self.

Nothing will impede
The ocean of her
Bounty.
Nothing can contain her.
There are no rules to hold her
magnificence.

So love her irreverence,
Improvisation,
Improbable victories.

Love her brashness,
Her bold,
Her rougher edges.

Open your arms in gratitude
For all she risks
To crack us open

That we may each
Ever more deeply
Freely
Be.

I Know A Woman

I know a woman
who is exhausted.
She works midnight hours,
carving out the time she needs
from days given twice over
to all who require her care.

She forgets to put herself
into her own arms,
neglects to feed
the very woman who feeds
all other need.

I know a woman
who is climbing Kilimanjaro,
19,000 feet of unstoppable courage,
but does not fully know
her own majestic light.

I know a woman
who is wrenched with
too many
good-byes
in too short a time
whose heart
burns daily for
all who are in pain.

I know a woman
who is banishing fear,
ushering it
out of her house.

It held sway
one too many years.
Now she is done.

I know a woman
who has found
an empty room.
She is scrawling on the walls.
She is splashing paint.
She is making noise.
She is dancing a fiery dance.
She is willing to fail.

I know a woman
who quit her job,
and every day
makes friends
with her unknown.

I know a woman
who holds us
with prayer.
I mean prayer that can change your life.

I know a woman who is enraged,
pain stitched in her pockets,
tears carried too long,
who now must
open her mouth
and sing
or shout or
speak her truth.

I know a woman,
a warrior queen
whose
little girl
heart
needs a lullaby.

I know a woman who
cracks herself
open
open
open
to be boundless love,
a priestess of raw devotion.

I know a woman
who lost her son
and gained her voice
to let loose a fury of light
upon the world.

You know a woman.

We know a woman,
struggling
to grow her radiance,
the flame of her heart
burning away
who she is not.

Our stories together
hold back the darkness.
Our struggles together
wrestle fear into light.
Our bodies together listening,

breathe a breath
that forges the new.

So yes.
And yes.
And yes.

Let's rally to birth the light.
Buoy one another,
Stand fully alive.
Let us breathe upon the flame.

There is no longer time
to sit alone at the kitchen table
and weep
for a fractured world.

The doors of our hearts
are swinging open.
We are calling to one another
arms outstretched.
We are joining hands.

The birth cry of the new world
is a song sung by women
silenced for centuries
heard again
now
when we gather
in the name of light.

Oh women,
Blind me with your radiance.
Bear witness to one another.
The time has come.

We have everything to give
to a world that
needs nothing more
than
our
fierce
present
love.

Let Yourself Love Her

(to be read aloud)

I was waiting in line
biding my time,
waiting for my friend
who was late
for our date,
when I looked up to see—

Beauty

like a splash of
cold water
walk by me.

You know what I mean,
like some kind of goddess
walked in.
And there she was,
unaware
how everyone
had stopped to stare.

And I felt myself
crumple
like grey seeping in,
counting the years
brimming tears,
feeling late,
out of date,
wanting to hide,
reside elsewhere.
But this is what I thought:

Just let yourself love her.
Don't be caught
in your own
self-loathing.
Don't try to criticize
her face, her form,
her clothing.

Just love that beauty
exists like this,
beauty abounding,
resounding,
confounding.

Celebrate how the light in the room
changed,
how people were rearranged
by this grace, this face, this space
of light created.

It's killing us
this self-critique,
body hatred,
feeling bleak.

Don't cut her out.
isolate,
judge yourself,
medicate.

Just open to her.
Open to YOU.
You wild gorgeous flower,
shine that right through.

Say hello.
Soften your heart.
Say yes
to her beauty,
soak it in and
take part.

On This Day

Written for the TedX Olympic Boulevard Women and all who
gather in the name of growth and love

We might have gone
grocery shopping
on a day like this,
picked up a dozen eggs,
Reynolds Wrap, green apples.

We might have stared at a screen,
cleaned the basement,
folded clothes,
sat on the couch,
bored, fearful, hesitant.
We might have taken a nap.

But today is a day we've been waiting for.
Today is a day for fiercely loving who we are.
Today is a day to rock our worlds.

Today we meet
the eyes of other women,
feeling our our own nervous stomachs,
held breath,
certain doubt.

What can I give?
Do I have what it takes?
Am I too much?
And do I dare?

But we take a deep breath.
We know why we've come.

On this day we choose to gather.

On this day we choose together
to build a life electric in truth,
fiery in courage,
steeped in compassion,

A life that leaves our bodies singing
with a gift only we can give.

We come to hear ourselves in one another,
to recognize each step we take alone
builds momentum for us all.

We choose to gather.

We choose together
to stand in vulnerability
cheer our neighbor
love more.

A woman's heart is a vast plane
upon which a horse can run,
say the Tibetans.

And do you know the strength of yours?
Immeasurable.
Can you feel its light?
The light of ten thousand suns.

Do you see these women?
Grace in motion.

Blessings rain down on a day like this.

On this day,
no ordinary day,
on this day,
as we gather
Together.

For Women Who Gather

*Dedicated to all the women who have attended
my Radiant Life Retreats*

Even after staying up until the wee hours celebrating with you—eating chocolate strawberries with our eyes closed, showering one another with love, telling truths— I have awoken early. And my heart is beating in a quiet new way.

In these early hours, I want to say a few things to you about moving out into the world again after our nestled, crazily courageous, reigniting time together. I'm feeling like a mama, a sister and a best friend all rolled together. So with all the love in my heart, I ask you:

Be exquisitely gentle with yourself. You have all opened to the glimmer of something new. You have said hello to a *you* you'd forgotten about or didn't know was there at all or had forgotten how gorgeous and awesome she was. You've stretched and welcomed her. She is exquisitely beautiful. You are exquisitely beautiful. Be gentle with yourself when that new tender part seems to leave the room, when your old familiar self shows up in full technicolor and reinstates herself claiming her territory. She might say, "But you've *always* been shy or sad or merging or invisible." She might even say, "Did you really think you could change? Did you really thing a day or two could change you?" At which point, just look at her with the kindest eyes and take the deepest breath you can, wrap your arms around her and love her. Soon enough your new, tender brave self will come to sit beside you again and tell you more of her secrets.

One of the great mysteries of life is why once we open do we ever close again? Why, once we have stretched to a new sense of self, a new beauty, bravery, artistry, a new love for ourselves and the world—why do we ever constrict and collapse and grow numb? Once we've tasted vastness, why do we choose boundary? But we do, my dear loving women, and it's okay. Because we never ever return to the exact closure we started with. It's softer around the edges. There's light shed upon it. There's sometimes even a little humor or self-compassion. Yes, our heart, our bodies, will constrict again. But once we've tasted, seen, touched a beauty rare and fine, we know it is as close as a a full-bellied breath of self-compassion and courage. We know the door is there and we have a key, our very own key that unlocks the threshold. We won't always choose to use it, because we will be tired and doubtful and busy and distracted. But once we've really bowed down to the mystery and power of our own beating hearts and realize how it contains the kingdom (or the queendom) of our own generous thriving, it's hard not to go back and visit more often.

Carry these women tangibly in your heart. Every day, let a moment of breakthrough find you smiling as you drink your morning tea. I don't need to tell you to remember. It will happen. But I do need to tell you to take note when one of these beautiful women comes to mind. She's there with yet another gift for you. She's there giving you a gentle nudge in the direction of your greatest heart's unfolding. Receive her fully and sit with her for a time. She's the angel of your day.

Let's promise together to do some small thing daily that marks our beauty and our value, that fills us with delight. Let's put on a scarf and think how beautiful we look. Buy a flower bouquet and set it on our desks. Take a breath and notice the softness of our bodies. Write a love letter to ourselves in whatever way we can, each day. Let's do it because we will not only be lifting ourselves but every woman in this circle.

And then, yes, everyone we meet will be perceptibly changed because we chose an act of beauty on this particular day.

I love you. And it's not personal. And it is personal. And even if those words hold a charge, hold resistance, even if you have somehow decided that you can't love someone you just met or that you can't love someone you pass on the street or that something happened in your life and you decided you couldn't trust loving, even saying the words, even if all of those or any of those things are true—I love you and I will stand in that vulnerability and tenderness always. I love the buds of you, the blossoming of you, the courage of you, the tenderness of you. I love you in your total stuckness and your huge moments of freedom. I beg of you to not reserve your love for only those you'd call your intimates. When you can, make the world your beloved. We're all climbing our mountain and daring to unfurl our hearts. Let them sing. Let them love unbounded. You will never regret loving more. You will never regret cracking open with the immensity of your love. You will only begin to dimly hear all the other daring I love you's whispered, shouted, proclaimed, sung, wildly danced that are growing us, growing this beautiful humanity, growing this planet into our truest nature—singing and spinning as unconditional, ceaseless, boundless love.

Inches Away

I want to be quiet inside and a wild roar in a room when needed. I want to be loose and sometimes wobbly in all the right places so when it comes time to stand up and tell the truth, I know how vulnerable and uncertain feels. I want to look in a mirror and say, "Ah yes, this is where we are in life's great unfolding." I don't want to sigh. I want to laugh with how juicy life can look. I want to be an ocean of transformation. I want to invite you in, to swim in unexpected currents, to feel briskly alive, to be rocked to sleep. I want to envelop you with blue and brush back the hair from your forehead and hold you, buoy you, so you can breathe the sun while you lay in my waves.

I do so love to love you. And YOU is vast. You are my lover and my children, and my dear pal in Brooklyn. YOU is my just met beautiful friend whose secrets will be new to me but whose texture is ancient and familiar. You is a man on the radio who makes me hold my breath because what he says scares me. But I want to be a woman who can love us into radical awakening, who believes that love can do that, who fiercely breathes in what is ugly, digests it and keeps only what can evolve into light. I want to be the woman who includes myself in that love I freely give, whose own laughter evokes the girl in me full of dreams and delights and possibilities. I want to love myself into lightness, to lay my burdens down, to do things daily that make my whole body happy.

Listen, I wake up sometimes an aching pile of bones and I look in the mirror and think "And my husband still loves this?" And I formulate a list of all that is broken and I reel my way through my day from coffee to red wine and coffee again. And I feel behind in all of life's accomplishments.

But this story is rapidly growing old.

I am inches away from owning it all with a fierce joy. I want to open my body wholly to be touched by the world. I am moments away from being ceaselessly awake, awake to what is really going on, awake to the beauty that is miles beyond skin deep. I am seconds away from knowing that living is art, is beauty, is a gift. I am so close to timelessness that I don't care how old I am, because I am 13 and 83 right now and I am yearning and innocent and wise all at once. And mostly I am willing, willing to be open to the miracles that can happen in an instant, changes that can unfold overnight. I am willing to be someone new, right now, right here, with this very breath.

SIX

Becoming the Song

Twenty Days

Handel wrote the Messiah in twenty days. Twenty days. That's less than three weeks. When in the thick of it, he forgot to eat or drink. Even sleep. Can you imagine? Can you imagine that kind of bliss, the bliss of being so captured by what needs to move through you—through *you* specifically—that you forget yourself? May we all have twenty days as rich. And if we had only twenty days like this, would it not be enough? I feel giddy at the thought. Twenty days of allowing something exquisite to pour through. Twenty days of softening the boundaries of self to allow a gift to burn through and emerge for the good of many. Twenty days where our daily needs are not so needed because the Soul is being fed and is giving its gift. I want this for myself. I want this for you. I want this for all of us.

Yesterday, I worked with a yoga teacher who asked me to imagine that the light above my head was a burning candle and that the beauty of the flame atop my head was like a fiery crown and was filled with passion and purpose. Then, she asked me to let it burn, to let it burn through the top of my head, over my face, pouring down my neck to land as a flame at the center of my chest, surrendering all until its arrival at my heart.

We need to melt into our gift. We need to burn into our offering. We need to stand in the fire of creativity and receive what wants entry. We are gorgeous bodies that are best when empty, ready to dance with what is greater and always available. But so often, so many days besides those twenty days, we are too full. We are full of self-doubt, to-do lists, guilt, lethargy. Sometimes if we are lucky we are full with joy or appreciation or gratitude. But that kind of fullness always leaves room for more goodness, more movement—possibility. The dark fullness is thick with immobility.

Fire burns it away. Passion. Recognition of our gift. Even quietly beginning to claim the tiniest part of what we are here to do lights the fire. Dear God, why do any of us wait to strike the match? My whole body yearns for those twenty days when everything disappears but blinding light, where the next step is never taken alone, where we've joined forces with a greater storm of livingness and where we offer ourselves moment to moment to carry it, write it, scribble it, paint it, build it. We offer ourselves as conduits for life more abundant. We offer ourselves to the being of beauty that is alive and breathing and waiting to converse with any fiery heart that is ready.

There can be no more waiting. Twenty days could begin tomorrow. Three weeks of burning and yielding and offering. Every NOW is the moment to begin.

Becoming the Song

She paints the walls of the loft daily. She climbs ladders to paint the corners where the walls meet the ceiling. There is light everywhere in the morning. The sun streams through the huge back window. It paints the concrete floor with its warmth. She drinks tea and paints and sometimes scrawls pieces of poetry, written in pencil, under the paint, over the paint. It's for her. No one else need know these offerings of her heart. Not now. It's her practice. It's her practice to move the words from deep inside her onto the canvas, onto the walls of the home she has chosen for herself. The words she writes and the paint she spreads speak to the walls and ask that they not only keep her safe but that they open like wings to the vastness that she already feels growing in her body, the vastness that she knows can no longer be contained. It has already been asked to stay in such a careful, small space for too long.

She knows the vastness. It's no mystery to her. But she knows how quiet she must be with herself, how she must gently woo herself out of the closures she has known. Sometimes she wakes in the night and climbs ladders in her nightgown. She plays a song over and over and loses herself in its invitation. She dances on the ladder, almost flies, in the stream of moonlight.

No one comes to see her. She is not sad. She is swimming in the sacred. Her pencil wears down to a stub and soon she chooses charcoal. There's no hiding what she has to say now and she's ready for it to be seen, first by her eyes only—until her whole body can celebrate the Self she sees all around her, until her whole body says YES to what she creates.

Then she already knows, she'll open the door, the walls will fall away. She'll keep playing the song and it will somehow lift her out into the street, her own little universe of Self and her skin will be the walls she has painted and the poems will fall from her lips and her feet will leave wet footprints like she just walked out of a vast ocean of fluid self and decided she was ready for a concrete walk down the block. She'll meet the eyes of every one she passes with her simple gaze, a gaze that offers the stars and the yes and the tears and the breaking free and the closures falling like sparkler magic all around her feet.

She won't go home because she has become it. She will walk now. She will walk on. The music will play. Her heart will beat the rhythm of the song she has become.

Wholeness

My little son
turns his head,
his smile lighting up
the distance
between us.

He sits in a kayak
his father behind him
eager to begin the journey.

Both wear
brightly colored life jackets,
hold long wooden paddles.
Both are buoyant.
Father and son.
Father and sun.

"Have fun!"
I smile,
a little nervous to send them out
even on this small loop
around the bay.

It's one of a thousand partings
that quietly cracks me open,
a mother's practice for good-byes
yet to come.

They push out,
paddle in unison,
following a line of sunlight
into the blue.

Now they are beyond my reach,
now almost out of sight.

I am standing at the shore
and also
somewhere timeless,
a familiar ache
rooting me to this spot,
as if my standing
could prevent future loss.

Finally,
the call of a white egret
returns me.

I turn and walk back to a quiet house.

Something in the light of the sky,
or the way my body merges
with the heat,
or something in my heart beat
echoing my feet upon the earth,

something soothes
the quiet ache and I find myself
enveloped in a wholeness,
a wholeness that holds all who part,
a wholeness that knows no parting,
a wholeness that feels only the timeless
embrace
of love.

"Love List"

by my daughter, age 10

The "i" in list is dotted with a heart,
the list numbered to 37.

We're celebrating
our friend's birthday.
She asks us to write
her age in love.
What do we love?
Who do we love?
We each ask 37 times.

'Love list'
by my daughter
open now on the table,
two days later,
beauty blazing
off the page.

It beckons.
I breathe.

Number one. Family
Number two. Friends.

She said otherwise those two would take up all 37 slots.

Piano
Animals
Roller Coasters

Choclete.

Spelled
C-H-O-C-L-E-T-E

holidays
babies

She's the pied piper.
a baby whisperer.
They follow her everywhere.

Number 9 Acting
Number 10 ME!

ME! she writes.
ME!

Not a single person over
10 writes ME!

ME! with an exclamation point.
Me! I love myself.

All parenting worries quiet for now.

Summer
Laughter
Love
Cupcakes
Tea
Sleep
Bare feet

Her eternal summer self before me.

writing
fire
earth
air
water

elements raining, blazing, holding, lifting her.

snow
skipping
hugs
tickling
cuddling

oh this precious time, a decade chock full,
my lap open to her curling just a little longer

clouds
smiling
art
the heart

and yes yes yes still this

stuffed animals

learning
excitement
rain

Chocolate chip cookies
and *Erin*,
our birthday friend.

Oh dear child.
My 10 year old girl.
My wise little one.
Your list of love.
Your love list.
Your love.
You.

Lineage of Beauty

She,
the daughter
who brings to life
a fading cardinal
with a brush of red on the wing,

the bright bird
now sings
on the side of her mother's
weathered mailbox.

She,
the daughter
whose eye
insists on beauty
wants her mother
to see again
the good cheer, apple red,
hope of spring.

I, the daughter
of she who paints
the red bird
hear her delight
in all that fly.

"Look here,"
she says.
"Quickly."

"Goldfinch
Blue Jay
Red-winged black bird."

117

"Don't let beauty pass
without your notice."

"White egret
Red-tailed hawk
Nut cracker
Chickadee."

She,
the daughter of one
who yearned for flight
but couldn't leave.

I,
the daughter of one who
loves Amelia—
she who dared to fly.

My daughter,
the one who stands
in a lineage of women—
women who name the beauty
that sets us free,

now discovering
her own unbridled vastness
in which to fly.

The Plane of The Heart

With a deep bow to Sofia Diaz and her lineage of teachers
(to be read aloud)

Don't think of your heart
as lodged in your chest
pumping away
with never a rest.

Think of it this way
Or better yet feel it:

The heart is a plane,
and feeling reveals it.

It's a vast field of grace
beyond time, beyond space
reaching out
and extending,
love never ending,

no boundary
or limit.
It lives you.
You live it.

Soak in its sweetness,
Sheer completeness.

Don't abstract it.
Contract it.

Just stand in stillness
arms extended

Nourished by its nectar.
Conduct the heat,
hear the beat,
Be a love detector,
Reflector,
Projector.

Let it eat you.
Devour you whole.
Dissolve in the light
a radiant soul.

We live in a world
that dismisses
the subtle.
What we feel
sense,
intuit
is lost in the shuffle.

Reclaim it.
Sustain it.
Stop, stand and feel.

You're held aloft by that plane
and the heart plane is real.

Feel your heart in your finger tips.
the sensation on your lips,
compassion shining from your hips.

Drip with love.
Soak in it.
Saturate.
Steep.

Then offer that love,
let your whole body weep.

Wake up to what's real
And what's real is this:
The heart rules the queendom,
The heart, love and bliss.

Everything that's not bliss,
it's what's leaving you now.
You're shaking,
You're sobbing,
let your body allow

something much greater
to live you today.

Offer is up,
Find a new way.

Know you are vast,
And that love doesn't cease.
It cascades from your heart
as you stand
and increase
the peace.

Freedom Yet To Find

If there's a shred, ounce
scrap, swath, field
of freedom yet to find,

set me on that course,
put me on that plane

(though fear of flight
reduces me
to quivering flesh).

I will board,
lunge from boredom,
assume makeshift wings,
say farewell to what's known,
invite
the impossible,
the implausible,
the improbable.

If there's a pool, galaxy,
snippet, cup
of freedom yet to find,

Bring it to my lips
let me drink
though I may shrink,
stumble
or disappear.
I will consume
what scares me
and know

the magic of peacock
who gobbles
red ant poison
but walks unscathed
as beauty.

What is known is always knocking.
You do not have to answer.
Fling open the back door
to the YES
of unspeakable light
and boundless time.

The invitation ever exists—
if there is a hint,
whiff, touch,
whisper of freedom
left to find,

Ready your ship.
Let the winds blow.

Refuse the map of
discovered worlds.

Let love be your compass.
Set sail.

BIG
LOVE
TO EACH
AND EVERY
ONE OF YOU.